Pe

Written and illustrated by

Val Biro

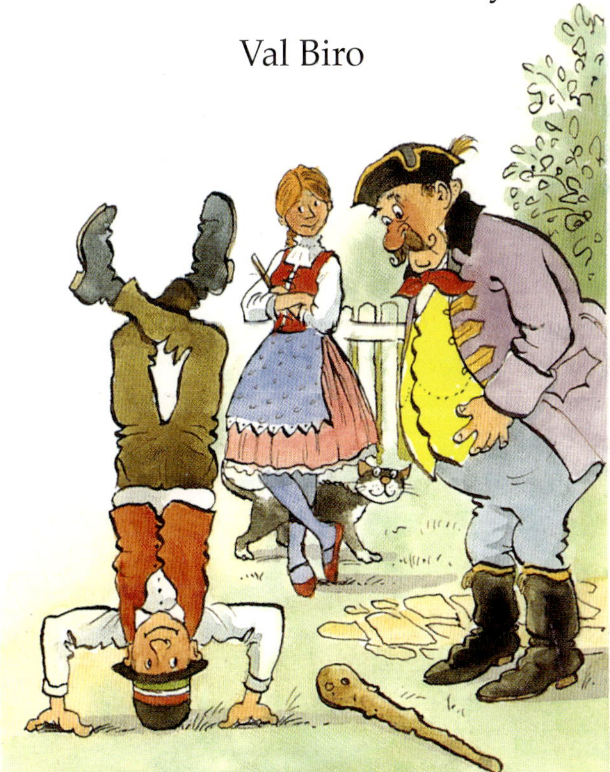

Ginn

Once there was a man called Peter. He was a cheerful young man and he liked a good joke, especially the kind that fooled others. And if he made a little money while he was fooling them, so much the better. Although he was an amusing fellow, there was no doubt that he was just a common crook, and people called him Peter Cheater.

Peter had become quite famous in the little town where he lived. "Look out, here comes Peter Cheater," people would warn each other. "You'd better hang on to your purse!" They never knew whose turn it was to be tricked next. But Peter was always so polite when he played his tricks that most people were taken in before they knew what had happened.

3

Peter lived in a small cottage with his young sister, Esther. Ever since their parents died, they had lived by themselves, sharing the cooking and keeping the cottage as clean as a new pin. Esther, like Peter, enjoyed a good joke. She laughed at her brother's tricks and antics. And she was always on hand to help, especially when his jokes resulted in money. Well, they had to live on something, didn't they?

In a big house at the other end of town lived the Mayor. A fat and bad-tempered man he was, and as greedy as could be. He had plenty of money, but he always wanted more. He always wanted the best of everything just for himself, no matter what. Although he was very grand and very important, there was no doubt that he was just a silly old fool.

He had heard of Peter and his tricks. The town was full of stories about how Peter had cheated everybody and anybody. The Mayor had heard these tales and was determined that one day he would put this trickster into prison. But first, he would test Peter himself. "I'll catch him out at his own game," he boasted, "and give him what for!" The townspeople sniggered when they heard this and waited to see what the old fool was up to.

They didn't have to wait long. One day, as the Mayor was riding down the High Street, he came face to face with Peter Cheater himself. Now we'll see some fun, thought the people.

The Mayor stopped his horse in front of Peter and addressed him in a grand way.

"Good morning, my man. We meet at last. I understand that you are a bit of a crook, that you play tricks on honest men, that you cheat ordinary decent folk, that you make fools of your elders and betters."

Peter bowed with a flourish. "And good morning to you, Sir. I'm afraid you flatter me. I only make fools of those who let me."

"We'll see about that! I am the most honourable, decent, *extra*ordinary man in this town and very much your elder and better. Can you for one moment pretend that you could fool and cheat *me* as well?"

"Why certainly, Mr Mayor," replied Peter cheerfully. "Of course, I can." He paused for a moment for some quick-thinking. "Of course I can," he repeated, "but I need something to cheat you with, and I can't find it in this town."

The Mayor became curious. "This thing, where *can* it be found, may I ask?"

"Half a day's walk from here, Mr Mayor," replied Peter.

"Half a day's walk?" the Mayor echoed. "Does that mean half a day there and half a day back? Do you mean to keep me waiting for a whole day before I can see what you can do?"

The Mayor began to lose his temper. "That's nonsense!" he raged impatiently. His curiosity had got the better of him and he wanted action here and now. Suddenly he had an idea. "Here," he said to Peter, "take my horse. It will get you there and back in no time."

He got off his horse with much huffing and puffing and handed the reins to Peter. Peter struggled into the saddle, pretending he didn't know which end of the horse was which. First he sat on its neck and then on its rump, much to the merriment of the crowd. Even the Mayor laughed in his superior way, as Peter rode away holding on to the horse for dear life. Once he was out of town, though, he settled into the saddle like a real soldier.

He reached the neighbouring village soon
enough. It was market day and people were
bustling about, busily buying and selling. A
farmer noticed Peter and the fine horse he
was riding. He had an eye for a bargain and
asked Peter for the price.

"A thousand crowns with his tail," said
Peter. "Or a hundred without," he added
craftily.

The farmer scratched his head. He could make no sense of this. "I see you don't understand," said Peter and took a deep breath. "Let me explain. If you buy the horse, tail and all, the price is a thousand crowns. If you buy the horse without his tail, the price is one hundred crowns and you can ride it away. However, should you prefer to buy the tail only, without the horse, put nine hundred crowns into my hand and the tail is yours."

"In that case," said the farmer, who wasn't born yesterday, "I'd rather take the horse without the tail."

"Done!" said Peter and he promptly produced a pair of scissors from his pocket and snipped off the horse's tail. Putting it under his arm, he pocketed the hundred crowns, shook hands with the farmer and was off before you could say Peter Cheater.

13

Peter ran and ran until he reached the lake outside the village. Without taking off his clothes, he waded right in until he was waist deep in water. Then he planted the horse's tail into the mud and wedged it firmly with a couple of large stones. Having done that, he smeared himself all over with mud, came ashore and limped all the way back to the Mayor, pretending to be in great distress.

The Mayor burst out laughing when he saw Peter. He laughed till his fat stomach heaved and the tears ran down his cheeks.

"What's happened to you, my boy?" he asked at last, wiping his eyes.

"Don't ask me, Mr Mayor, Sir," wailed Peter. "Please don't ask! What a disaster! You know well enough that I can't ride, but somehow your horse and I got to the village. I was just breathing a sigh of relief when that wretched horse bolted and jumped straight into the lake! Only by sheer luck and some clever swimming did I manage to scramble out. But unfortunately the poor beast is dead."

When the Mayor heard this, he stopped laughing at once. He choked and went purple in the face.

"I don't believe a word of it! It can't be true! You can't cheat me as easily as that! You are a liar!"

"Mr Mayor," protested Peter, "why should I lie to you? Please go and see for yourself, Sir, if you can spare the time. The horse's tail is still sticking out of the water. And if I don't speak the truth, then by all means send me to prison."

The Mayor calmed down at these polite words. "Very well," he said, "lead me to the lake."

"Me, Sir? But how can I?" burst out Peter, his face a picture of misery and pain. "How can I possibly go with you now, Mr Mayor, with all my bones broken? In truth, I am more dead than alive."

So the Mayor ordered a couple of his soldiers to come with him and search for the horse. Sure enough, when they got to the lake, the first thing they saw was the horse's tail sticking out of the water.

"There's my horse!" cried the Mayor joyfully. "So Peter wasn't lying after all. Let's help the poor beast. Perhaps he isn't dead yet."

He was so pleased to see the tail that he waded in himself, leaving the soldiers on the shore. He grabbed the tail and tugged with all his might. He tugged and tugged until, finally, the two heavy stones gave way.

The tail flew out of the water and the Mayor went SPLASH! flat on his back in the mud. "That crook," he spluttered as he tried to get up and scramble ashore. "That crook's cheated me after all! He'll suffer for this if he lives for a hundred years! I'll … I'll … I'll … fling him in jail … I'll lock him up … I'll put him in chains till he rots!" He raved on and on, swore and threatened, waving the tail in his clenched fist.

Meanwhile, back in the town, Peter Cheater was having a fine time with his friends at the Inn. He had money in his pocket after all, so why shouldn't he be enjoying himself? But when he happened to glance out of the window, he saw the Mayor coming along, horsetail in hand, covered in mud from head to foot and followed by a jeering crowd. Peter had to think fast.

"Landlord!" he called. "Bring me five more bottles of wine. Here's the money. Now, whatever I do next, just say that the bill's been paid. Do you understand?"

The landlord didn't understand at all, but he nodded eagerly and pocketed the money. Just then the door burst open and in strode the Mayor.

"Come in, Sir, come in," invited Peter with a welcoming smile. "And do please seat yourself at my table, Mr Mayor."

"Certainly not!" thundered the Mayor. "I haven't come to drink with the likes of you, but to fling you in jail as you deserve. Now, pay for your drink and come at once!"

"Right away, Sir," said Peter obediently, and called the landlord. "What do I owe you, Landlord?"

The landlord played his part well. "You had five bottles earlier, and five just now," he said. "That makes ten bottles in all, if I'm not mistaken."

"Quite correct," said Peter. With that he took off his hat and threw it on the floor. Looking at the landlord with a sly wink, he asked, "Well, Landlord, does this settle my bill?"

"It certainly does, Sir," replied the landlord.

The Mayor stood stunned. He promptly forgot all about the mud and his horse, though he was still holding its tail. He stared at the landlord, he stared at Peter, he stared at the greasy hat on the floor.

"What kind of hat is that?" he asked
suspiciously.

"A very special kind," replied Peter
proudly. "It's the kind of hat that pays my
bill when I throw it down, Mr Mayor."

23

The Mayor was overwhelmed with curiosity. He sat down at Peter's table to question him further. "And where did you get this miraculous hat, my man?"

"Oh, I inherited it from my old dad," replied Peter.

"And tell me," continued the Mayor, "has it been of much help to you?"

"Why, Mr Mayor, I would have died of thirst and starved to death many a time without this hat of mine. I always wear it when I go out. Then I eat and drink to my heart's content. When it comes to paying the bill, I throw it down and hey presto, the bill is paid!"

The Mayor went green with envy. He wanted that hat for himself. Think of it! To eat and drink as much as you want and not a penny to pay. What a hat!

"I want to buy your hat," he croaked.

Peter shook his head. Oh no, he couldn't ever think of selling it. Whatever would his old dad say? But the Mayor insisted. "Sell it, my son. Please sell me this wonderful hat. A hundred crowns should do it."

Peter burst out laughing. "What are you thinking of, Mr Mayor? A hundred crowns for a miraculous hat that will pay without question? Do you take me for a fool, Sir?"

"I'll give you another fifty. Let it be a hundred and fifty crowns," pleaded the Mayor.

"Let it be nothing, Mr Mayor," said Peter, "because I won't sell my hat."

"I could spare two hundred," went on the Mayor.

Peter pretended to hesitate, and when the Mayor offered a further hundred crowns, he said, "Well, Mr Mayor, if you want my hat so badly, I give in. The hat is yours."

The Mayor was overjoyed. He jumped up, pressed the three hundred crowns into Peter's hands, grabbed the hat and ran out, grinning from ear to ear.

On his way home he called on all his friends and neighbours and invited them to be his guests for dinner at the most expensive restaurant in town. That evening, the guests came to the Mayor's house. There were at least a hundred of them, all dressed up in their best finery. When they were all assembled, the Mayor placed the hat carefully on his head and announced, "We are ready. Let's go!"

The guests followed him, but the greasy, crumpled old hat amused them so much that they couldn't help laughing. The Mayor would have none of this. "You won't laugh so much when you see what this dirty hat is capable of doing. My word you won't!"

The guests were curious to know more and plagued him with questions, but the Mayor shook his head. "You'll know at the proper time," was all he said.

So off they trooped to the restaurant. It was such an expensive place that every dish came at double the price. But the Mayor assured his guests that price was of no concern and urged them to treat themselves royally. The guests accepted his advice gladly. They ate and ate until the larder was empty. They drank and drank until the cellar was empty too. Having emptied both larder and cellar, they were well content to go home.

The Mayor summoned the head waiter
and asked for the bill. It took a long time to
add it all up, but eventually the head waiter
presented it to the Mayor. The Mayor only
smiled when he looked at the enormous
total. He then took off his hat and winked
at his guests.

"Now then, my friends, you shall see
what this hat of mine is capable of!" And so
saying, he threw the hat down so vigorously
that it raised the dust on the floor.

"Well, Head Waiter," he demanded
triumphantly, "is the bill paid to your
satisfaction?"

31

The head waiter smiled, but shook his head. "Of course it isn't, Sir. How could it be?"

The Mayor thought that perhaps he hadn't thrown the hat properly, so he picked it up and dashed it down again. The effort made him quite pink in the face. "There! Surely the bill is settled now, isn't it?"

The waiter smiled even more broadly and shook his head even more sadly.

What could the Mayor do? He threw the hat down for a third time, so hard that it nearly fell apart. Quite red in the face he asked again, "Surely you can't say that the bill isn't paid this time, can you?"

"I certainly can," replied the head waiter gravely. "You haven't paid a single crown so far, whereas the bill comes to five hundred."

It was then that the Mayor realised how cruelly Peter had cheated him again. Quite purple in the face, he paid the bill and ran back to the Town Hall. He commanded two soldiers to come with him and arrest Peter for his crime.

Peter Cheater was at his cottage, preparing the table for the dinner that Esther was cooking at the stove. The stew smelled delicious and the pot was boiling and bubbling nicely.

Esther was just about to serve up the stew, when she happened to glance out of the window. What she saw nearly made her drop the pot. In the distance was the Mayor, marching angrily towards the cottage, followed by two grim-faced soldiers. "Peter, look!" she blurted. "It's the Mayor!"

Peter had to think fast. "Quick!" he cried, "Give me that pot!" He grabbed the hot pot, raced outside and placed it on top of a tree stump. Then he sat down and began to stir the bubbling stew with a ladle, pretending to taste it from time to time.

The Mayor soon arrived—and he was so astonished by what he saw that his mouth flapped open and he gasped like a fish. Of course he gasped, for there was Peter cooking a stew that was boiling and bubbling away on a tree stump *without* a fire underneath! The Mayor had never seen anything like it and the sight made him forget all about his horse or the hat.

"How ever do you manage to do that, my man?" he asked.

"What, Mr Mayor?" said Peter, trying to look innocent.

"To cook a stew without a fire."

"Oh that," answered Peter modestly, and explained. "You see, Mr Mayor, this pot is three hundred years old. Many, many stews have been cooked in it during those three hundred years, and in all that time the pot has become so used to cooking that now it can do so without a fire."

"What a remarkable pot!" marvelled the Mayor.

"It certainly is," agreed Peter. "I've had many pots in my time, Sir. Some were prettier and some bigger, but they were all ordinary pots. They took no notice when I threw in the meat and onions and potatoes, until I lit a fire under them. Now this pot, Mr Mayor, this pot begins to warm itself as soon as it sees the first piece of meat. I wouldn't part with it for all the money in the world!"

The Mayor wanted that pot. He wanted it more than anything else. He was so envious that he burst into tears.

"Why are you so sad, Mr Mayor?" asked Peter.

"I am sad to hear that you won't part with your pot. I was about to offer a hundred crowns for it."

Instead of replying, Peter took a ladleful of stew and held it under the Mayor's nose. "Taste it, Sir," he said invitingly.

The Mayor swallowed the stew and smacked his lips. It was good. Very good indeed.

Peter said, "Now you see, Mr Mayor, the kind of stew my pot can cook, and all without a fire. I can tell you honestly that if by chance someone offered me three hundred crowns for it, I would still hesitate."

39

"Peter, my boy," cried the Mayor, "I am that somebody. You can have the three hundred crowns."

Peter pretended to hesitate. At last he spoke.

"It is lucky for you, Mr Mayor, that you are the Mayor. If you, Mr Mayor, weren't the Mayor, I wouldn't part with this pot for four hundred crowns. But since you are the Mayor, Mr Mayor, you can have it for three hundred."

"I will never forget your generosity, my son," said the Mayor gratefully. He paid the three hundred crowns, took the pot and hurried home, went straight to the kitchen and placed the pot in the middle of the floor. Then he ordered his servants to cut up the meat, peel the onions and potatoes, throw them into the pot and cook a stew.

"Here on the floor?" asked the Cook.

The Mayor nodded. "Certainly, right here on the floor."

The servants stopped peeling. They stared at the Mayor in a curious manner, with raised eyebrows, as if he were not quite all there.

"Why do you stare at me like that?" demanded the Mayor. "Do you take me for a fool?" He laughed. "You are the fools, let me tell you, if you can't see that this is a miraculous pot which cooks without a fire! Don't you believe me? Just wait and see."

The servants said nothing. They just waited to see. But they saw nothing except a pot full of stew that wasn't cooking.

"Is it cooking?" asked the Mayor.

"It isn't," replied the Cook.

"Perhaps," hesitated the Mayor, "perhaps it needs more air. We must blow."

So the servants blew. The Mayor, too, squatted down and blew until he was red in the face, but no matter how much they blew, the pot refused to warm up.

The truth struck the Mayor like a thunderbolt. That crook Peter had cheated him again! He groaned and his face went quite white. He jumped up furiously and shot out of the kitchen. He ran straight back to Peter's house to arrest him and fling him into jail.

Peter strolled out of his cottage with a broad smile. "It's good to see you again, Mr Mayor," he said, welcoming him.

"You'll soon see what's good," roared the Mayor. "I'll fling you in jail. I'll put you in chains. I'll keep you locked up for the rest of your miserable life! Then you'll see what's good, my man!"

Peter looked at him in mild surprise. "What could possibly have happened, Mr Mayor? It's not an hour since we parted in the greatest of good friendship."

"I'll tell you what's happened," croaked
the Mayor. "That wretched pot of yours is a
fake. It won't cook. It won't even warm up.
That's what's happened!"

Peter laughed till the tears ran down his cheeks. "Of course it won't cook! Not without this tree stump which you left behind." And he dropped the stump at the Mayor's feet.

The Mayor gasped in astonishment. "Is that what's missing?" he asked.

"It is, Mr Mayor. I was about to bring it over to you to make sure that you wouldn't think I was cheating."

The Mayor was already reaching for his purse, delighted by Peter's explanation. "How much, my boy?"

"The stump is worth nothing by itself, Mr Mayor. But to give you the pleasure, you may have it for a hundred crowns."

The Mayor paid up, heaved the heavy stump onto his shoulder, and made for home. People lined the street as he staggered on, and laughed at the sight.

"Stump up, Mr Mayor! Stump up!" they jeered.

He was in a great sweat by the time he reached home. Dropping the stump on the kitchen floor, he placed the pot on top of it, and sat down to wait for the pot to boil. He could have waited for ever, because, of course, it didn't boil. It remained stone cold.

This time the Mayor was so angry that he said nothing. All he was able to do was to grind his teeth. But he ground them so loudly that the whole town echoed with the sound, and Peter heard it too.

He went into the cottage and called Esther.

"Take this tin whistle, my dear," he told her, and explained what she was to do with it. Then he took down his grandfather's hat—the one with the seven linings—and put it on. His preparations complete, Peter sat down by the front door to wait for the Mayor.

The Mayor arrived sure enough. He stopped in front of Peter. He said nothing, he just ground his teeth. Each time he ground them, Peter nodded.

"You are quite correct, Mr Mayor. What you think is perfectly true."

"And do you know what I think?" ground out the Mayor.

"Yes, Sir. You think that I am the biggest crook in the world."

The Mayor stopped grinding his teeth because his mouth dropped open in surprise. "How did you know?" he asked.

"Because I am indeed the biggest crook in the world."

"And what else am I thinking?" pursued the Mayor.

"That this time you won't have mercy on me."

The Mayor was impressed. "I must say that's very bright of you!"

"I can be even brighter," replied Peter and produced a stout stick. He pressed it into the Mayor's hands. "Mr Mayor," he said, "I am sure you'd like to hit me over the head. I admit that I've cheated you badly and I deserve it. So here I am, there's the stick, please hit me." He adjusted his grandfather's hat—the one with the seven linings—and waited.

The Mayor needed no prompting. He gritted his teeth, swung the stick round and THUMP! brought it down so hard that Peter collapsed like an empty sack.

When Esther saw this, she came out of the cottage and blew the tin whistle three times. As she blew it for the third time, Peter sprang up and rubbed his eyes. "Oh, I have enjoyed that nap," he said and stretched himself.

"You'd have slept till Doomsday if the whistle hadn't woken you," said Esther.

This was too much for the Mayor. "Do you mean that that whistle can wake you up, even after such a blow as I gave you?" he asked in wonder.

Peter smiled knowingly. "Oh yes," he said, "and even without a headache!" And he stood on his head to prove it.

The Mayor began to shake. He wanted that tin whistle. He wanted it so badly that he began to tremble. "Please sell it to me," he begged Peter. "I've been yearning to have such a whistle all my life."

Peter played along for a while, saying that it was an heirloom and he couldn't part with it, but the Mayor insisted. At last, they struck a bargain. The Mayor would give a thousand crowns and two saddle-horses for it. No sooner said than done, they shook hands and the Mayor ran home to fetch the money and the horses.

"Well, Esther, my dear," said Peter to his
sister. "Let's go in and pack. I think it's
time we went."

Esther and Peter packed up everything
neatly. They had just finished when the
Mayor came running with the horses and
the money. Peter pocketed the money, took
the horses' reins and handed over the tin
whistle. "Here you are, Mr Mayor, but may
I suggest that we try the whistle to make
sure I haven't cheated you yet again?"

"Very well," said the Mayor, "but how?"

"I suggest that I hit you over the head with the stick, Mr Mayor, and that my sister blows the whistle. Now, if by any chance you don't revive, Sir, then it's clear that I've cheated you and I shall repay everything. But if you do revive, Mr Mayor, then all's well!"

The Mayor agreed. So Peter took the stick, swung it round and THUMP! brought it down so hard that the Mayor collapsed like an empty sack.

By the time he came round, Peter Cheater and Esther were miles away!